Canada Close Up

CANADIAN SPORTS

Susan Hughes

Scholastic Canada Ltd.

Toronto New York London Auckland Sydney
Mexico City New Delhi Hong Kong Buenos Aires

Photo Credits

Cover (left) © Lisovskaya/Dreamstime.com; (right) ©
Diademimag/Dreamstime.com; (lower) David Boily/AFP/Getty Images
p. iv: Dave Reede/Firstlight
pp. 2, 14, 15, 26, 27, 32, 41: istock
p. 3: Firstlight/brandx
p. 7: CP Photo/Toronto Star, Peter Power
p. 10: Hockey Hall of Fame
p. 11: Doug MacLellan/Hockey Hall of Fame
p. 13: Gerry Thomas/National Hockey League/Getty Images
p. 16: Dr. James Naismith Basketball Foundation
pp. 18, 35: The Canadian Press/Adrian Wyld
p. 20: Neil Hodge/Neil Hodge Photography/Synchro Canada
p. 22: Ringette Canada
p. 28: The Canadian Press/Chris Young
p. 30: Nicolas Asfouri/AFP/Getty Images
p. 37: Ian Walton/Getty Images Sport/Getty Images
p. 42: The Canadian Press/Ryan Taplin
p. 43: The Canadian Press/Paul Chiasson
p. 45: Paul Bereswell/Hockey Hall of Fame
p. 46: Mark Ralston/AFP/Getty Images
p. 47: The Canadian Press/AP/Matt York
p. 49, 53: Canada's Sports Hall of Fame
p. 50: The Canadian Press/AP/Itsuo Inouye
p. 56: Frank Lennon/Toronto Star
p. 58, 59: Dave Sandford/Hockey Hall of Fame

Library and Archives Canada Cataloguing in Publication

Hughes, Susan, 1960-
    Canadian sports / Susan Hughes.

Includes index.
ISBN 978-0-545-99012-7

    1. Sports--Canada--History--Juvenile literature.
I. Series: Canada close up (Toronto, Ont.)
GV585.H83 2009   j796.0971   C2008-905169-6

ISBN-10 0-545-99012-2

6 5 4 3 2 1   Printed in Canada   09 10 11 12 13

Mixed Sources
Product group from well-managed
forests and other controlled sources
www.fsc.org Cert no. SGS-COC-003098
© 1996 Forest Stewardship Council
FSC

Table of Contents

Introduction

Canadians love sports!

Canada has two official national sports: lacrosse and hockey. But we play all kinds of sports. We've even invented some! Not only do sports help keep us fit, they're also fun.

Let's get moving! Together, we'll find out more about what sports mean to Canadians.

Chapter 1

Canada's National Sports

There are many popular sports in Canada. But there are two that are special to Canadians: lacrosse and hockey.

Each one has a long tradition in this country. Each has become important to our culture.

Lacrosse

For centuries, First Nations peoples, such as the Mi'kmaq and **Six Nations**, played a special game. It was similar to today's lacrosse.

In 1994 the government passed a bill that made the national summer sport of Canada lacrosse, and the national winter sport hockey.

The men played it for spiritual reasons. They played it to settle arguments about ownership of territory. They also believed that it taught them skills that would help them prepare for war. And they played it for fun, of course!

Two teams faced each other on the field. The players held wooden sticks with leather netting. They tried to throw a ball made of deerskin, wood, clay, stone or another material into the other team's goal. They played on fields that were up to several kilometres across. Sometimes hundreds of warriors — or even up to a thousand — played at once!

About 500 years ago, Europeans came to this country. It is said that French explorers saw the game being played and thought the wooden stick was similar to the staff carried by a bishop, called a **crozier** (or *acrosse*). They may have named the game after the stick, *la crosse* or lacrosse. However it came about, the name stuck.

The sport became popular with settlers who came to Canada. By the late 1800s, lacrosse clubs had been formed in every province from coast to coast. The game is still popular in Canada and is played in many countries around the world.

Canada has three professional lacrosse teams, including the Toronto Rock, seen here playing the Rochester Knighthawks.

Today, the game is played with titanium or aluminum sticks. These have plastic heads and mesh in which rubber balls are caught and thrown. It's fast-paced and exciting and is known as "the fastest sport on two feet."

The International Lacrosse Federation wanted to recognize the role of the Haudenosaunee Six Nations Confederacy in inventing the game of lacrosse. They accepted them as a full-member nation. Their team is the Iroquois Nationals. It plays in the top division along with teams from nations with much larger populations, such as Australia, the United States, Japan and, of course, Canada!

Hockey

No one really knows where and when the game of hockey was first played. Was it England, France, the United States, Holland or Canada?

In the 1800s Europeans brought many hockey-like games to Canada, such as Irish **hurling** and Scottish **shinty**. Hockey probably developed from these games over the years, but no one really knows where. Perhaps it was Canada. But if it was, no one can agree exactly where in this country it first was born.

Nova Scotia, Quebec and Ontario all claim to be hockey's birthplace. There are records of hockey being played in Kingston, Ontario, and Halifax, Nova Scotia, in the 1870s. The first recorded set of hockey rules was written by James Creighton in Montreal in 1875. There were only seven rules! And players would try to hit a wooden puck into the opponents' net. Modern hockey had begun!

This photograph, taken around 1920, is one of the earliest photos of a hockey game being played.

The original cup donated by Lord Stanley

The game became very popular. It became part of the annual Montreal Winter Carnival. But there was no trophy for the winning team. So, in 1892, Lord Stanley, the Governor General of Canada, donated a bowl which would be used as a trophy. This became the Stanley Cup, which is now presented annually to the winning team in the National Hockey League.

By the late 1890s, there were hundreds of hockey teams in Canada, and many in the United States. In the 1900s, equipment, such as skates and pads, began to be made just for hockey. Some of the rules changed and many were added. The game became faster. The shots became harder. Players began to wear helmets. Goalies began to wear masks. Hockey became even more exciting to play and even more fun to watch.

Hockey is Canada's most popular sport. More Canadians play, watch and volunteer at hockey games than any other sport. Hockey is truly a national sport of Canada!

Calgary Flames fans show their support in a sea of red jerseys.

One in five Canadian adults plays hockey.

Chapter 2

Made in Canada

Not many of the sports we play today have actually been invented. Most usually develop from other sports over time, like hockey. It got its start from games that began in other countries.

But some of these sports have been perfected in Canada. There are even some sports that were invented, from scratch . . . by Canadians!

Basketball

Did you know that basketball was invented by a Canadian?

🏀 James Naismith

In 1891 James Naismith was teaching young men at a school in Massachusetts in the United States. Naismith believed good health was important — both of the mind and the body. But when winter came, students were bored with traditional indoor games. So Naismith worked to make up a new one.

In his game, skill and speed were more important than strength and power. He challenged teams of competing players to throw a soccer ball through a peach basket that hung high up on the side of the gymnasium balcony. He came up with thirteen rules. For example, players could not carry the ball for more than a few steps unless they bounced, or "dribbled," it. Also, they could not tackle the other players. This way, no one would get hurt on the hard floor.

The game was a hit. It is now one of the most popular games in the world.

🏀 **Chris Bosh of the Toronto Raptors tries to make a basket.**

Synchronized Swimming

Water ballet has existed in many parts of the world since ancient times. In the 1920s along came Canadian Margaret Sellers, a diver and water polo player. She helped develop a style of swimming called "ornamental swimming" by combining swimming and skills taught by the Royal Life Saving Society. Music was added, and this became synchronized swimming.

Synchronize means "to happen at the same time." When swimmers perform acrobatic moves in the water "in synch" with music and each other, either alone, in pairs, trios or teams, they are doing synchronized swimming.

🐬 A pair of synchronized swimmers perform their moves.

The sport requires strength and endurance, grace and flexibility, and split-second timing. It demands excellent water skills. It also helps if you can hold your breath for a really long time underwater!

How do the swimmers stay in synch with the music when they're underwater? Underwater speakers help them hear the music clearly.

Floor Hockey and Ringette

What do the two sports have in common? They were both invented in Canada by Sam Jacks.

Jacks was the assistant physical director at the West End YMCA in Toronto in 1936. That is where he invented floor hockey and set down the first set of rules for the sport.

From 1948 until 1963, Jacks was the director of Parks and Recreation in North Bay, Ontario. He noticed that girls weren't playing much hockey. He thought they might enjoy having a different team sport they could play on ice. So, in 1963, he set out his first set of rules for ringette. After two years of polishing, the rules were finalized.

Ringette looks very similar to hockey.

The sport became very popular with women. It is now played in all ten provinces and three territories in Canada. The sport is also played in many countries around the world, such as Finland, Sweden and the United States.

Ringette is a team sport. Each team has six players on the ice at a time. This includes a goaltender. Players use a straight stick, without a blade, to pass, carry and shoot a rubber ring to score goals. The players' size and ability to **stickhandle** is not as important as their skating, agility and hand-eye coordination.

Five-pin Bowling

By the early 1900s, ten-pin bowling had been in Canada for decades. Bowlers rolled heavy balls down lanes, trying to knock down ten pins which stood at the end of them. Tommy Ryan had opened the first ten-pin bowling alley in Canada. But bowlers coming to his Toronto Bowling Club complained that the balls were too heavy and that it took too long to play — especially when some of the bowlers were trying to squeeze in a game over lunch!

> **Five-pin bowling is not played in any country other than Canada.**

Ryan began to experiment. He took five pins and asked his father to whittle them down to three-quarters their original size. He found a smaller hard rubber ball, one that could fit in his hand. He rolled it down the lane at the five smaller pins. The game of five-pin bowling was invented!

Today at least half a million Canadians play the game every year.

● Tommy Ryan's Toronto Bowling Club

Chapter 3

Popular Sports

We all have a favourite sport that we like to take part in or watch. But some sports are more popular than others.

Soccer

What sport do girls and boys play most in Canada? Soccer! It's also the most popular game in the world. Maybe that's because all you need to play is a field and a soccer ball! Sometimes soccer is called "the beautiful game."

⚽ Soccer is becoming more and more popular in Canada.

There are two teams in soccer. Players try to put the ball into the opponents' net. Players (aside from the goaltender) cannot touch the ball with their hands or arms on purpose. They can kick it, or they can hit it with their head.

Some soccer players are amazing at using their feet . . . in the air! One of the most famous soccer players in the world, Pele from Brazil, has invented a "bicycle kick." With both feet in the air, higher than his head, he moves his legs in a pedalling motion to move the ball backwards. It takes lots of practice to be as skilled as someone like Pele!

In the United States and Canada, the game is called soccer. In other countries, it is called football.

Every four years, countries from around the world take part in the largest soccer championship in the world, called the World Cup. During this time in Canada, you might see people's homes or cars adorned with flags showing the country they support. Soccer really is a world sport!

⚽A player attempts a bicycle kick

Swimming

Many people in Canada swim. Swimming is the second most popular recreational activity in Canada. It's a good way to relax and get a good workout!

You can swim indoors or outdoors, in pools or lakes. Many children take swimming lessons to improve their skills. They learn how to do several popular swimming strokes, such as the backstroke, breaststroke, and front crawl. They challenge one another to races. They compete to see who can do the goofiest dives or the most underwater somersaults in a row.

Many children also enjoy swimming competitively. In fact, competitive swimming is the third most popular sport among children in Canada after soccer and ice hockey.

🌊 Swimming can help you do other underwater activities, like snorkelling.

Knowing how to swim means you are safer around the water. But it is always important to wear a lifejacket when you are in a boat.

Snowshoeing

Snowshoes were invented by Canada's First Nations peoples. The special shoes helped them travel through deep snow more easily. When European fur traders and settlers came to Canada, they began using snowshoes, too.

In the 1800s settlers no longer used snowshoes just for getting places. They snowshoed for fun! In fact, in the 1870s, snowshoeing was one of the most popular sports in Canada. Many people joined snowshoeing clubs, especially in eastern Canada. Snowshoers would meet for many activities, including races and hurdling. They would go on tramps together at night. They would even slide down hills on snowshoes.

Each club, or region, had a particular colour. For example, Quebec City clubs were red; snowshoers from the Trois Rivières district wore white; Montreal snowshoers wore blue.

> The Montreal snowshoe club formed in the early 1800s. It was one of the first athletic clubs in North America.

Canadian football

Canadians love to watch football. It's our second most popular spectator sport. The rules of Canadian football are similar to those of American football, but there are some differences: the Canadian football field is larger than the American field, and Canadian teams have 12 players on the field, while American teams have 11. Canadian football also has 3 **downs** instead of 4.

In both games, players try to run with a football and score in the other team's "end." To prevent their advance, defending players try to block them or tackle them to the ground. Offensive players can also kick the ball for extra points.

◆ The Saskatchewan Roughriders battle it out against the Winnipeg Blue Bombers during the 2007 Grey Cup.

The championship game of the Canadian Football League is the Grey Cup. It is the largest sporting event in Canada and is the most watched sports event in Canada. Every year, about 4 million Canadians watch the game!

Many young Canadians play flag football. Most flag football leagues do not allow blocking or tackling. Instead, the defensive players must remove a flag from the ball carrier to end the play.

Curling

Curling began in Scotland. The first curling game in Canada was played by a Scottish regiment stationed here in 1789. Now Canadians are the best curlers in the world!

◎ **Curling is one of the most popular sports in Canada.**

There are more than 750,000 curlers in Canada, more than in any other country in the world. Estimates show that Canada has three-quarters of the curlers worldwide. Not only are there lots of them, but they are extremely talented. The Canadian men's team has won 25 out of 41 world championships.

Two teams have four players each. The players from each team take turns "throwing" the curling rock down the length of the ice. The rock is made from special granite. They throw it toward the "house," a bull's eye painted at the end of the rink.

Two players follow the rock. They carry brooms. They may sweep in front of the rock to make it go faster or to change its direction. Once each team throws eight rocks, the "end" is over. Only the rocks in the house count in the scoring, and only the team whose rock is closest to the centre of the house — the button — gets points. That team gets one point for each of its rocks that is closer to the button than the opposing team's closest rock. After ten ends are played and scored, the game is over.

Curling has been described as "chess on ice." Strategy is a big part of the game.

Extremely Popular

Canadians like extreme sports, too! What makes a sport extreme? Usually it means the sport involves danger, such as high speed or great heights, or spectacular stunts. Some great examples are **motocross**, **in-line skating** and **BMX** biking.

Snowboarding is very popular with Canadians. Boarders enjoy "carving" down the hills, as well as trying to reach high speeds and learning to perform tricks both on the snow and in the air. Many ski clubs provide special terrain parks with half-pipes, rails and jumps, so boarders can test their skills. In 1998 slalom racing and half-pipe riding snowboard competitions were added to the Winter Olympics.

Chapter 4

Great Athletes, Great Moments

We have a lot to be proud of. Here are some great moments and great athletes who had us jumping up on our feet to cheer!

Wayne Gretzky

Wayne Gretzky was skating before he was three years old. At 17, he was playing professional hockey in the World Hockey Association. When the Edmonton Oilers joined the NHL in the 1979–80 season, he scored 51 goals — the youngest player in the NHL ever to reach 50. By the time he stepped off the ice for the last time, "The Great One" had broken many records — 61 of them, in fact. For example, he won the Hart Memorial Trophy (for the player most valuable to his team) ten times — more than any other player. His number, 99, was retired throughout the NHL in 1999. Wayne Gretzky is without a doubt the most famous Canadian athlete of all time and perhaps the best hockey player ever.

Chantal Petitclerc

Chantal Petitclerc is one of the greatest athletes in wheelchair racing. She began racing in 1987 — and finished last in her very first race! Since then, she has worked hard to achieve  an incredible record. She won five medals in the 2008 Beijing **Paralympics**. Altogether, the superstar won 21 medals in five Paralympics. Petitclerc retired in 2008.

Steve Nash

Steve Nash moved to Canada from South Africa when he was two years old. After getting involved in many sports, including soccer and hockey, he discovered basketball. He was a natural. He is

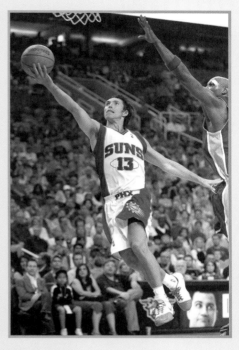

now Canada's most famous basketball player. He is ranked as one of the top players in the National Basketball Association's history for three-point shooting, free-throw shooting, total assists and assists per game. He was a four-time NBA All-Star for 2002, 2003, 2005 and 2006. And he also won the Most Valuable Player award two years in a row, in 2005 and 2006.

Tom Longboat

Although Tom Longboat's amazing achievements happened a long time ago, he remains one of Canada's most famous athletes and best long distance runners. Born on the Six Nations of the Grand River reserve near Brantford, Ontario, 19-year-old Tom Longboat shocked people by winning the 20-mile Around the Bay race in Hamilton, Ontario in 1906, almost setting a new record. Ten days later, he won the 15-mile Ward **Marathon** in Toronto. Two months later, he won the 10-mile Christmas Day Race in Hamilton, breaking the Canadian record by two and a half minutes. People were stunned. Who was this new athlete nobody had ever heard of?

Then he did the incredible: he won the Boston Marathon in 1907, smashing the record by 5 minutes. Longboat died when he was 61, but he is still remembered for his remarkable feats.

Cindy Klassen

Can you imagine winning a gold medal at the Olympics? How about two silvers? What if you won those three — and another two bronze medals, for good measure!

This is what Cindy Klassen, world-class speedskater, has done. The all-around athlete took up speed-skating when she was 18. It was not her favourite sport, but she decided to give it a try. She was a natural. Klassen competed in the Salt Lake City Olympics in 2002 and won a bronze medal. At the Turin Olympics in 2006, Klassen won an incredible five medals: a gold (in the 1500-metre), two silver (in team pursuit and 1000-metre), and two bronze (in the 3000-metre and 5000-metre). This is the most medals ever won at one Olympics by a Canadian. Altogether, she has won more Olympic medals than any other Canadian.

Marilyn Bell

On September 8, 1954, 16-year-old
Marilyn Bell stood on the shore
of Lake Ontario. She was on the
American side, at Youngstown, New
York. It was 11:00 p.m. She was
planning to be the first person ever
to swim across Lake Ontario. Two
other women were also trying to
make the same marathon swim
that night.

Bad weather conditions forced Bell
to swim much farther than she had
expected. But Bell was tough and
experienced and outlasted her
opponents. On September 9,
shortly after 8 p.m., Bell reached
the opposite shore, becoming the
first person ever to swim across
Lake Ontario. In 1955, she became
the youngest person to swim

across the English Channel, and in 1956, she swam across the Juan de Fuca Strait that separates Vancouver Island and Washington State. Bell was inducted into Canada's Sports Hall of Fame in 1958.

Summit Series, 1972

It is 1972. An eight-game hockey
series between Canada and the
Soviet Union is beginning. Canadian
fans believe they have the best
hockey players in the world and that
the series will be a walk in the park.
The first four games are played in
cities across Canada. Fans are ready
for their professional players to crush
the Soviet amateurs. But in the first
game, the Canadians are defeated 7
to 3. They win the second game, but
the third ends in a tie. Fans are
stunned. When Canada loses Game 4
in Vancouver, the players are booed
off the ice. Phil Esposito, a centre for
the Canadians, tells fans that they
are trying their best. He is shocked
that they would boo their own team.

The final four games are in Russia. In Game 5, once again, Canada loses. But things start to improve for the Canadians. They win the next two games. The series is now tied!

The final game is played on September 28. Fans across Canada turn on their televisions, some staying home from work. Teachers roll televisions into school gyms so students can watch this historic end to the series. The country seems to hold its breath waiting to see if their team can win.

At 12:56 in the third period, Canada ties the game at 5. Both teams fight hard in the final minutes to win. And then, incredibly, with 34 seconds left Paul Henderson scores. Canada has won!

Paul Henderson celebrates his winning goal.

Hockey has been changed forever. From now on, it will be a faster, better game, thanks to the challenging Russians. And Paul Henderson's final goal will go down in Canadian history as the most famous goal ever.

Women's and Men's Hockey, 2002 Winter Olympics

It was February 21 in Utah, site of the 2002 Winter Olympic Games. The Canadian women's team was facing off against the United States team in the gold medal match. The Americans had beaten the Canadians in the Nagano Olympics, four years earlier in Japan. They were coming into this game undefeated all season. They were favoured to win.

But the Canadian women had other things in mind and when they took to the ice, they turned up the heat. Although the Americans had more power-play time, the Canadians took many more shots.

By game's end, their team also had more goals. The Canadian team won 3 to 2 and went home with their first Olympic gold medal.

Perhaps the Canadian men's team was inspired by the women's success. Also facing an American team and playing for gold, the men won their match 5 to 2. It was the first time a Canadian men's hockey team had won an Olympic gold since 1952.

Across the country, crowds took to the streets to celebrate Canada's domination in the sport that continues to mean so much to them.

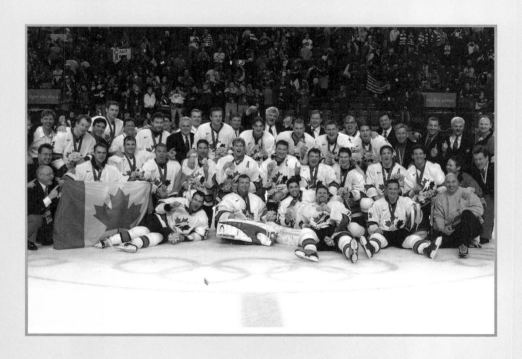

Glossary

BMX (bicycle moto-cross): an organized bicycle race that takes place on a dirt track

crozier: a hooked staff carried by a bishop

down: an attempt in football to move the ball ten yards

hurling: an Irish game similar to lacrosse played with a broad-bladed, netless stick

in-line skating: skates with two, three, four or five wheels arranged in a single line

marathon: traditionally, a cross-country foot race of 42.195 kilometres (26 miles, 385 yards); also means a difficult or long-lasting task

motocross: cross-country racing done on a motorcycle

Paralympics: an international competition for disabled athletes

shinty: a game derived from hurling, and resembling hockey, played in Scotland

Six Nations: a league of Iroquois tribes (also called the Haudenausaunee) which include the Mohawk, Oneida, Onondaga, Cayuga, Seneca and Tuscarora

stickhandle: to keep possession of a puck or ball by skilfully controlling it with movements of one's stick